Guest Spot

EIGHTIES [illegible]
Playalong *for* Trumpet

Wise Publications
part of The Music Sales Group
London/New York/Paris/Sydney/Copenhagen/Berlin/Madrid/Tokyo

Published by
Wise Publications
14-15 Berners Street, London W1T 3LJ, UK.

Exclusive Distributors:
Music Sales Limited
Distribution Centre, Newmarket Road, Bury St Edmunds,
Suffolk IP33 3YB, UK.
Music Sales Pty Limited
120 Rothschild Avenue, Rosebery, NSW 2018, Australia.

Order No. AM991067
ISBN 13: 978-1-84772-165-5

Arranging and engraving supplied by Camden Music.
Edited by Ann Farmer.
Compiled by Nick Crispin.

Printed in the EU.

CD recorded, mixed and mastered by Jonas Persson.
Trumpet played by Tony Fisher.

www.musicsales.com

Trumpet Fingering Chart

MOUTHPIECE

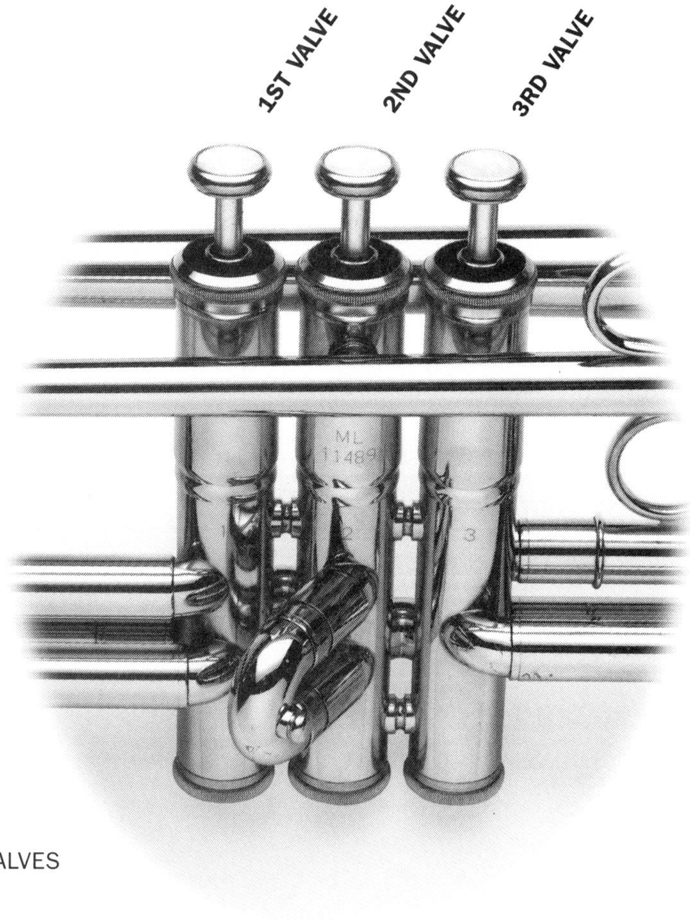

VALVES

Sounds: B♭ Trumpet, Cornet, Flugelhorn	Sounds: Baritone	Written	Right hand (valves pressed)
e	E	f♯/g♭	1, 2, 3
f	F	g	1, 3
f♯/g♭	F♯/G♭	g♯/a♭	2, 3
g ▶	G	a	1, 2
g♯/a♭	G♯/A♭	a♯/b♭	1
a	A	b	2
a♯/b♭	A♯/B♭	c^1	–
b	B	$c♯^1/d♭^1$	1, 2, 3
c^1	c	d^1	1, 3
$c♯^1/d♭^1$	c♯/d♭	$d♯^1/e♭^1$	2, 3
d^1	d	e^1	1, 2
$d♯^1/e♭^1$	d♯/e♭	f^1	1
e^1	e	$f♯^1/g♭^1$	2
f^1	f	g^1	–
$f♯^1/g♭^1$	f♯/g♭	$g♯^1/a♭^1$	2, 3
g^1	g	a^1	1, 2

▶ Indicates the lower limit of the best playing range

Transposition

The B♭ trumpet, cornet and flugelhorn sound a major second below the written pitch.
Rule: **Written C sounds B♭**

Written:  Sounds: 

The baritone sounds a major ninth below the written pitch. Rule: **Written C sounds B♭**

Written:  Sounds: 

Pitch System

The letter names which appear at the top of the fingering chart indicate the relative octave as well as the name of each pitch, as shown below.

C² B² C¹ B¹ C B c b c¹ b¹ c² b² c³ b³ c⁴ b⁴ c⁵

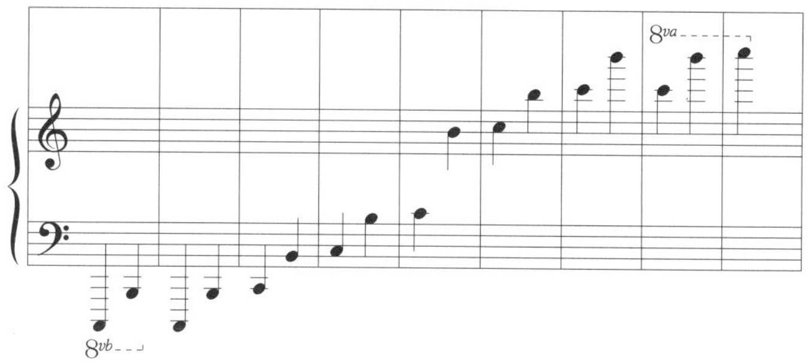

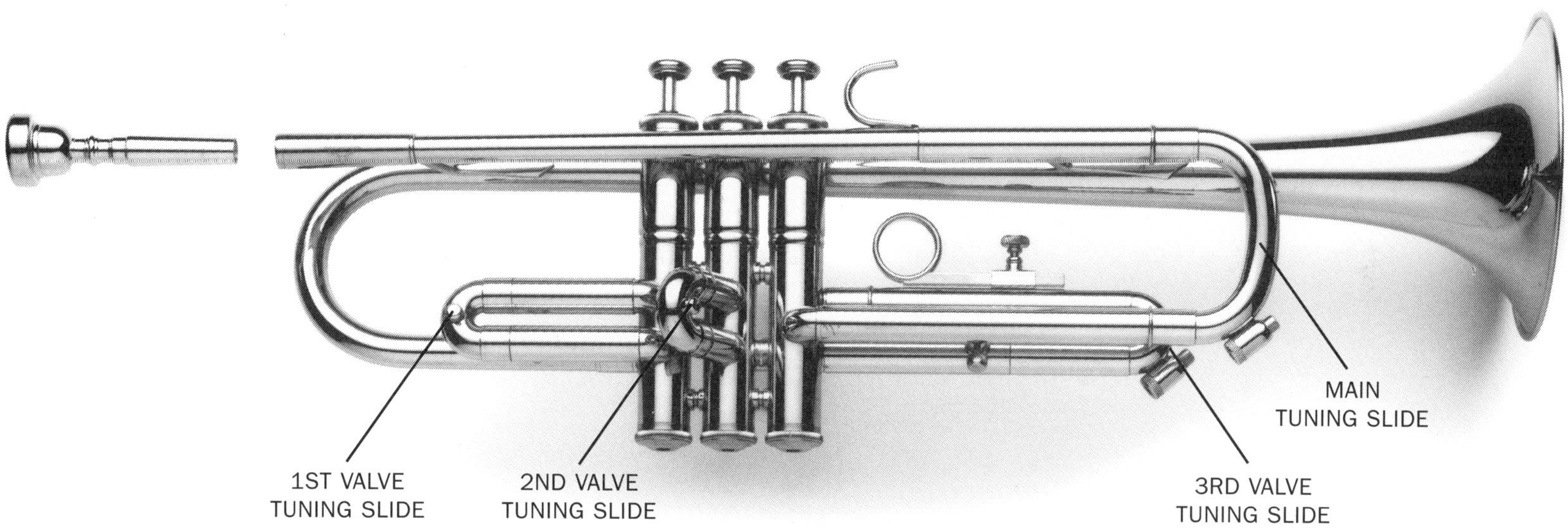

g♯¹/a♭¹	a¹	a♯¹/b♭¹	b¹	c²	c♯²/d♭²	d²	d♯²/e♭²	e²	f²	f♯²/g♭²	g²	g♯²/a♭²	a²	a♯²/b♭²	b²		c³	
g♯/a♭	a	a♯/b♭	b	c¹	c♯¹/d♭¹	d¹	d♯¹/e♭¹	e¹	f¹	f♯¹/g♭¹	g¹ ◀	g♯¹/a♭¹	a¹	a♯¹/b♭¹	b¹		c²	
a♯¹/b♭¹	b¹	c²	c♯²/d♭²	d²	d♯²/e♭²	e²	f²	f♯²/g♭²	g²	g♯²/a♭²	a²	a♯²/b♭²	b²	c³	c♯³/d♭³		d³	
1	2	0	1 2	1	2	0	1	2	0	2 3	1 2	1	2	0	2	1 2	0	1

◀ Indicates the upper limit of the best playing range

The Boy With The Thorn In His Side

Words & Music by Morrissey & Johnny Marr

35
f
mf
39
3
43
f
47
50
53
3
56
59
Repeat to fade
4

Don't Stand So Close To Me

Words & Music by Sting

34
38
1.2.
3.
3
Instrumental
mp
45
49
mf
53
mp
58
f
62
66
mf
70
Repeat to fade

Golden Brown

Words & Music by Jean-Jacques Burnel, Jet Black, Hugh Cornwell & David Greenfield

dim. poco a poco
dim. al niente
cue
cue
mp cresc.
Repeat to fade

I Still Haven't Found What I'm Looking For

Words & Music by U2

36
mf
39
3
43
46
49
3
52
f
56
61
Instrumental
9
f

73
3
3
76
3
80
84
88
92
mf
96
100
Repeat to fade
8

Live To Tell

Words & Music by Madonna Ciccone & Pat Leonard

mf
f
Rubato, slower
A tempo
senza sord.
mf

71
Instrumental
3
mf
78
81
85
mf
89
92
96
Fade to end
f

Man In The Mirror

Words & Music by Glen Ballard & Siedah Garrett

28
f
31
34
37
3
41
senza sord.
mp
44
47
cresc. poco a poco
50
54

57
f
61
64
f
67
70
73
ff
76
79
1.
81
2.

84
88
3
3
92
con sord. (straight)
p
mf
96
100
104
f
108
112
2
senza sord.
mf
dim. poco a poco
118
mp

The Power Of Love

Words & Music by Holly Johnson, Mark O'Toole, Peter Gill & Brian Nash

D.S. al Coda
Coda
con sord. (straight)
mp dolce
senza sord.

Take On Me

Words & Music by Morten Harket, Mags Furuholmen & Pal Waaktaar

to Coda
44
mf
49
53
57
D.S. al Coda
Coda
62
Instrumental
12
synth. cue
77
f
80
83

86
mf
90
94
98
f
103
109
115
121
Fade to end

Wonderful Life

Words & Music by Colin Vearncombe

Smoothly, with a relaxed feel ♩ = 106

29
più f
33
37
1.
41
2.
sax solo
7
mf
51
3
55
60
3

Optional
8va
più f
(8)
mf dim. poco a poco
sax solo to end

Who's That Girl?

Words & Music by A. Lennox & D.A. Stewart

43
47
D.S. al Coda
mp
Coda
52
56
3
mf cantabile
63
67
72
f pesante
78
mf
84
f cantabile
89
Begin fade
Repeat to fade

1 2 3 4 5 6 7 8 9

CD1 Track Listing

Full instrumental performances...

1. The Boy With The Thorn In His Side
(Morrissey/Marr) Warner/Chappell Artemis Music Limited/Universal Music Publishing Limited.

2. Don't Stand So Close To Me
(Sting) GM Sumner.

3. Golden Brown
(Burnel/Black/Cornwell/Greenfield) Complete Music Limited/EMI Music Publishing Limited.

4. I Still Haven't Found What I'm Looking For
(U2) Blue Mountain Music Limited.

5. Live To Tell
(Ciccone/Leonard) Sony/ATV Music Publishing (UK) Limited/Warner/Chappell Music Limited/EMI Music Publishing Limited.

6. Man In The Mirror
(Ballard/Garrett) Universal/MCA Music Limited /Warner Chappell Music Limited.

7. Power Of Love
(Johnson/O'Toole/Gill/Nash) Perfect Songs Limited.

8. Take On Me
(Harket/Furuholmen/Waaktaar) Sony/ATV Music Publishing (UK) Limited.

9. Wonderful Life
(Vearncombe) Hornall Brothers Music Limited.

10. Who's That Girl
(Lennox/Stewart) BMG Music Publishing Limited.

CD2 Track Listing

1. Tuning notes

Backing tracks only...

2. The Boy With The Thorn In His Side
3. Don't Stand So Close To Me
4. Golden Brown
5. I Still Haven't Found What I'm Looking For
6. Live To Tell
7. Man In The Mirror
8. Power Of Love
9. Take On Me
10. Wonderful Life
11. Who's That Girl

To remove your CD from the plastic sleeve, lift the small lip to break the perforations. Replace the disc after use for convenient storage.